DESERTS

A Buddy Book
by
Fran Howard

ABDO
Publishing Company

VISIT US AT
www.abdopublishing.com

Published by ABDO Publishing Company, 4940 Viking Drive, Edina, Minnesota 55435.

Printed in the United States.

Edited by: Sarah Tieck
Contributing Editor: Michael P. Goecke
Graphic Design: Brady Wise
Image Research: Deb Coldiron, Maria Hosley, Heather Sagisser, Brady Wise
Photographs: Animals Animals, Corel, Corbis, Digital Vision, Minden Pictures, Photodisc, Photos.com

Library of Congress Cataloging-in-Publication Data

Howard, Fran, 1953-
    Deserts / Fran Howard
        p. cm. — (Habitats)
    Includes bibliographical references and index.
    ISBN 1-59679-776-2 (10 digit ISBN)
    ISBN 978-1-59679-776-5 (13 digit ISBN)
        1. Deserts—Juvenile literature. I. Title. II. Series: Habitats (Edina, Minn.)

QH88.H575 2006
577.54—dc22

                                        2005031593

TABLE OF CONTENTS

WHAT IS A DESERT?

Deserts are dry land areas. Most deserts get less than 10 inches (25 cm) of rain each year. Most deserts are very hot.

A desert is one kind of habitat. Habitats are where plants and animals find food, water, and places to live. Different plants and animals live in different habitats.

The Sahara Desert is a hot desert. It is in Africa.

Deserts are located all over the world. Even though it is dry and hot, plants and animals live in deserts. Desert plants and animals are special. They do not need much water to live.

WHERE ARE DESERTS FOUND?

A view of the Sahara Desert's sand dunes.

Deserts cover about one-fifth of the Earth's surface. Deserts are found all over the world.

Most deserts are hot. But, some are cold. Antarctica is a desert that is covered by ice. The ice in Antarctica formed over thousands of years. The ice came from the small amounts of **precipitation** in this cold desert.

The Sahara Desert in Africa is the world's largest desert. It covers more than 3 million square miles (8,000,000 sq km). The Sahara Desert is very hot.

A view of the Gobi Desert.

There are many other deserts all over the world. Some of the most famous include the Kalahari Desert in Africa, the Mojave Desert in the United States, and the Gobi Desert in China and Mongolia.

THE DESERT CLIMATE

When people think of deserts, they think of sand. The Sahara Desert has many sand dunes. Still, most deserts have more rocks than sand.

Deserts are windy. They are also dry. Deserts are the driest places on Earth.

Sometimes, a rainbow forms after it rains in the desert.

Months or years may pass between rainstorms. But, sometimes it rains very hard in the desert.

One of the driest deserts is in South America. It is called the Atacama Desert. It can be many years before this desert gets even a small amount of rain. In some parts of the Atacama Desert it hasn't rained for more than 100 years. This is as long as humans have kept track of the rain there.

A view of Antarctica.

The hottest places on Earth are deserts. At night, **temperatures** can drop below freezing.

Some deserts are cold. There is a cold desert in Alaska. Antarctica is also a cold desert. Cold deserts have short summers and long winters.

DESERT PLANTS

Some deserts have few plants and animals. Others are rich in wildlife.

The cactus is a type of plant found in many deserts. Many animals get food and water from the cactus. For some, a cactus is home. The cactus wren makes its nest in a cactus.

The saguaro cactus is one of the largest types of cactus in the world. A saguaro can grow to be 60 feet (18 m) tall. This is taller than some houses.

The saguaro cactus grows in only a few deserts. One of these is the Sonoran Desert. This cactus grows very slowly. It may not grow flower blossoms until it is 40 or 50 years old.

Some saguaros weigh ten tons (nine t).

How Plants Survive In The DESERT

Plants need water to survive. Deserts are very dry. So, desert plants have special features that allow them to live in the desert.

There are many types of cactus that grow in the desert.

Desert plants have several ways to survive. Often, they do not grow too close together. And, some plants go **dormant**. This means they shed their leaves when it is dry. This helps prevent and reduce water loss. Other plants store water or grow very long roots.

The saguaro cactus is sometimes called "the giant cactus."

A cactus stores water in its roots and stems. It collects water in a couple ways.

A cactus has many short roots. This lets the cactus take in water when it rains.

Many desert plants have long roots. These roots grow deep into the ground. They grow until they reach water. The mesquite tree has long roots. Its roots can grow 80 feet (24 m) into the ground.

Many cacti have spines. The spines protect the cactus from animals. They also provide shade for the cactus.

Desert plants have special features that help them survive in heat.

DESERT ANIMALS

Foxes are desert animals. Foxes avoid the heat. They often come out at night.

Deserts have many different animals. Some animals eat plants. Some animals eat other animals. Desert tortoises, camels, and black widow spiders are a few of the desert animals.

The desert tortoise spends most of its life in a **burrow**. Adult tortoises can live for a year without water. Desert tortoises eat plants.

Desert tortoises find shade under rocks and boulders.

Camels also eat plants. A camel can even eat thorns with its tough mouth.

Camels store fat in their humps. They can go for five to seven days without food or water.

Camels have two rows of **eyelashes**. The extra eyelashes protect their eyes from blowing sand.

Camels have nostrils that close to keep out blowing sand.

Some camels have one hump. Other camels have two humps.

21

The rattlesnake is famous for its rattle. It shakes its rattle when danger is near.

There are also insects and reptiles in the desert. Black widow spiders are one desert insect. Their bites are **poisonous**.

How Animals Survive In The DESERT

Desert animals need water. They can die if they don't get enough of it. Many desert animals get water from the plants they eat. Others have special ways of storing water. Some are even able to make their own. The kangaroo rat's body can make water from dry seeds.

Desert animals can also die if they get too hot. Their bodies have special ways to keep cool.

Many desert animals avoid the hot sun. Some, like foxes and bats, stay out of the sun and heat during the day. They are awake and out at night. Bugs, rodents, and toads dig into the sand to stay cool.

The regal horned toad burrows under the sand.

The fennec fox has light-colored fur. This helps it stay cool. It also helps the fox to hide.

Many desert animals are a light color, such as tan. The lighter color helps desert animals stay cool. This color also helps the desert animals hide.

Lizards are a common desert animal.

WHY ARE DESERT HABITATS IMPORTANT?

People and animals need deserts for many reasons.

Desert animals and plants need each other. Together they form a **food chain**. Even the smallest plants and animals are part of a food chain.

Lizard

Mouse

Cactus

A rock climber in the desert.

Deserts supply many things that help people such as wind power. Also, some desert plants are made into medicine.

People like to visit the desert. They climb rocks, hike, and go dirt biking.

DESERTS

- The highest desert sand dunes are in the Sahara Desert.

- Desert lizards move quickly over hot surfaces. They stop to cool their feet in the shade.

- Sometimes, there are sandstorms in the sandy parts of a desert. A sandstorm is when wind blows the sand around.

- There is an area in a desert called an oasis. This area has water and fertile ground. Crops can grow there. Many people live in oases.

- Sidewinder snakes move sideways. This helps them move quickly on sand.

Important Words

burrow a small tunnel or hole in the ground where some animals live.

dormant something that is asleep, or not actively being used.

eyelashes hairs that grow on the edge of eyelids.

food chain the order in which plants and animals feed on each other.

poisonous containing a substance that can harm or kill.

precipitation rain, snow, sleet, or hail that falls to Earth.

temperature the degree of heat or cold.

Web Sites

Would you like to learn more about **deserts**? Please visit ABDO Publishing Company on the World Wide Web to find Web site links about **deserts**. These links are routinely monitored and updated to provide the most current information available.

www.abdopublishing.com

INDEX